The Womans Guide to Long Term Care & Elder Care Handbook:

Where we get it.
Who needs it.
Who pays for it.
What you need to do now.

By Don Grimes
© 2011 Don Grimes

Copyright © 2011 by Don Grimes
/Caregiver Generation
All rights reserved.

No part of this book may be reproduced or transmitted in any form or by any means without written permission from the author.

Printed in the USA

Introduction

Since 2002, my work has focused on creating and conducting public education programs on long term care and elder care nationwide.

I've given over 1,000 classes at organizations as diverse as Apple, HP, Qualcomm; States of Texas and South Dakota; University of Minnesota, Texas A&M, Michigan State University, Penn State University and Columbia University; New York Stock Exchange, Central Intelligence Agency and the Rand Corporation. In 2011, my firm completed the second nationwide long term care education effort for federal employees.

This book provides the essential information needed to be more effective in helping others while also planning for your own future care needs.

Help get this vital information out to your friends, associates and customers! You can sponsor copies of this book that are customized with your name. You or your organization can also become one of our Community Long Term Care Educators. Contact us at info@

caregivergeneration.com

Table of Contents

Chapter One:
Overview..7

Chapter Two:
What Is Long Term Care And Elder Care?...............11
Federal definition.......................................11
Physical limitation......................................12
Severe Cognitive Impairment..............................14

Chapter Three:
Where Do We Get Long Term Care Or Elder Care?........17
Nursing Home...17
Assisted Living Facility.................................19
Home Care..21
Adult Day Care...23
Hospice..24

Chapter Four:
Who pays for long term care or elder care?...........27
Health Insurance...27
Medicare...29
Long Term Care Insurance.................................31
Disability Insurance.....................................35

Medicaid..36

**Chapter Five:
Geriatric Care Manager**................................40

**Chapter Six:
Legal Considerations**....................................46

**Chapter Seven:
Conclusion and Review**................................53

Chapter One:
Overview of the Long Term Care/ Elder Care challenge

People today face an interesting "good news/bad news" situation. The good news is that we are living longer than ever. We can watch our kids and grandkids grow up. The bad news is that most of us will end up needing some sort of care and most of us will also be caregivers or actively involved in coordinating care for someone.

According to the dictionary "Elder Care" is care for older people. Elder Care is a subset of Long Term Care. Anyone at any age can need Long Term Care. So when we talk about Elder Care the information is fundamentally interchangeable with Long Term Care.

Today 25 million people are caring for someone over 50.

Past generations of Americans have been described variously as the "WWII generation", "Baby Boom Generation", "Millennium

Generation". Each generation has unique challenges.

Today people ages 25 to 65 are members of what I call the "Caregiver Generation" ™.

Their unique challenges:

1) Their parents, especially their mothers, are living longer and they will likely find themselves helping to care for their mom.

2) When the Caregiver Generation™ ends up helping an older relative they are likely adding this heavy challenge to a busy life already filled with work, financial and family challenges.

3) The Caregiver Generation™ themselves will enjoy record life spans, thus will have a higher chance of needing long term care themselves.

4) Most members of the Caregiver Generation™ do not want to be a burden on their children.

Chapter Two:
What Is Long Term Care?

When we think of long term care, we usually think of someone who is 100 years old, in a coma who is living in a nursing home. We would be right! That person does need long term care but they are not the typical person getting long term care today. Today only 18% of people get long term care in a nursing home.

Long term care is unique because there is a generally accepted definition of a long term care situation from a federal law passed in 1996 called the Health Insurance Portability and Accountability Act of 1996. This makes long term care less complicated compared to healthcare and health insurance, car accidents and car insurance.

There are two separate causes or "triggers" for needing long term care: physical limitations and severe cognitive impairment.

Physical limitation: The federal definition of long term care lists six "Activities of Daily Living" (ADLs) that we do every day (doctors, nurses or social workers usually refer to "ADLs"). The ADLs are:

1) Bathing: getting in or out of a tub or shower by yourself and washing your body in a tub, shower or by sponge bath; the ability to wash your hair in a shower, tub or in a sink.

2) Continence: controlling your bladder and bowel.

3) Dressing: putting on and taking off any necessary item of clothing.

4) Eating: getting food into your mouth, including use of utensils.

5) Toileting: getting on and off the toilet and the associated hygiene.

6) Transferring: getting in and out of a bed and chair by yourself.

We will officially need long term care when a licensed healthcare provider (MD, RN, PA) certifies that we need help doing at least two of the ADLs for a period expected to last at least 90 days.

Examples:

Example 1. Kevin and Ray each pick up a heavy box and hurt their back.

Kevin is in intense pain and ends up flat on his back on the sofa for 30 days. He misses work for 30 days and needs help with all six ADLs for the entire month. After 30 days of being hurt and miserable, he recovers and resumes his normal life.

Is this a long term care situation? The answer is no. It does not qualify because he was unable to do at least two of the six ADLs for only 30 days.

Ray hurts his back but not as bad as Kevin. However, his doctor says he cannot dress or wash himself for at least 90 days. Even though his injury is not nearly as bad as Kevin's injury (remember, Kevin could not do any of the ADLs for 30 days); the fact that Ray will not be able to perform at least two of the ADLs for at least 90 days makes his situation a long term care situation.

Example 2. Sue is a 75-year-old college professor teaching Mandarin Chinese to her students. Sue's brain and heart are healthy but she has severe arthritis in her hands and shoulders. For the last three years a retired friend has helped her each day with getting dressed and bathing.

Is this a long term care situation? Yes. Does it matter that Sue can still go to work every day? No.

The other "trigger" for long term care is when someone has a severe cognitive impairment that makes them a threat to themselves and others and is expected to last at least 90 days.

Cognitive impairment is defined as being disoriented regarding people, places, locations and time. Alzheimer's disease and stroke are common causes of cognitive impairment (there are two kinds of strokes, a "regular" stroke and a so-called "mini-stroke" or "TIA". "TIA" is short for Transient Ischemic Attack).

Standardized tests determine the existence of severe cognitive impairment. This diagnosis is commonly made by a neurologist, psychiatrist, psychologist or, in some states, a licensed clinical social worker.

There is usually little question about the inability to perform ADLs; someone becomes a quadriplegic after a car accident, someone with advanced dementia or an elderly woman who breaks her hip and becomes bedbound because it does not heal correctly.

Example 1: A 73 year old woman recovers at home for a week after minor surgery. Her pain medicine makes her forgetful to the point that she no longer recognizes family. Two weeks after the surgery her doctor changes the medication and the situation clears up. This is not a long term care situation because the cognitive impairment did not last 90 days.

Example 2: Your elderly mother stills lives in her own home. Nine months ago, she was diagnosed with Alzheimer's and began forgetting to turn off the stove and walking aimlessly for hours forgetting how to get home. This would be a long term care situation.

Chapter Three:
Where do we get long term care?

There are three places or "settings" people get long term care:

- Nursing Home (also called a Skilled Nursing Facility or SNF)

- Assisted Living Facility (ALF)

- At home or in the community

Today 80% of people get their care at home or in the community, 2% get care in Assisted Living Facilities and the remaining 18% in Nursing Homes.

Nursing Homes

A Nursing Home provides medical care to help cure or control an illness and has a RN onsite 24 hours a day. Therapy often comes from physical therapists, occupational therapists and speech therapists.

Residents usually are people recently discharged from a hospital and completing their recovery or people who will permanently reside in the facility.

Today more hospital patients are sent to Nursing Homes to recuperate and receive various types of therapy because it is cheaper than having them recover in a hospital.

Two groups of people permanently reside in a Nursing Home. One group is people with chronic (ongoing) conditions who need continuing medical treatment beyond that feasibly provided at home or in an Assisted Living Facility. The other group of permanent residents is people who need help but have no money and are receiving care paid by Medicaid. Some of these people may be physically able to live at home or in an assisted living facility. However, their Medicaid program may not pay for that level of care or if it does pay for home care or assisted living the benefit may be too low to be of practical use.

Choosing a Nursing Home

Medicare provides Nursing Home ratings at Medicare.gov; however, there is a limitation with government ratings. You can visit a highly rated facility and not like it; vice versa, you can visit a low-rated facility that is clean, good smelling and has happy residents. A facility's rating can be impacted by a single event on one day over an entire year. The recommended way to find a great facility is to visit it, do the "smell test" and talk to residents and their family.

Health insurance, Medicaid and Medicare typically pay for a semi-private room: two people in the room, unless a patient has a specific communicable disease. Most Nursing Homes allow a patient to pay extra for a private room.

If you are paying for the Nursing Home using your own money (called "private pay") you can pick any Nursing Home.

If Medicare is paying then the facility needs to be Medicare approved. If Medicaid is paying, they select the facility.

Nursing Homes come in many shapes and flavors. They can be stand alone, part of a hospital or associated with an Assisted Living Facility. They can be for-profit or non-profit.

Assisted Living Facilities (ALFs)

Assisted Living Facilities are a great option for people who like having their own place but don't want to be, or cannot be, entirely on their own.

Typically, ALF residents get an apartment with a kitchen, refrigerator and stove. ALFs either come pre-furnished or people can bring their own furniture. ALF staff can help residents with the Activities of Daily Living and provide housekeeping services.

There are two key differences between an Assisted Living Facility and a nice apartment building:

(1) Assisted Living Facility is required to have staff on site, and awake, 24 hours a day to help residents.

(2) Assisted Living Facility is required to offer three meals a day.

Many people in Assisted Living Facilities get over the depression and isolation they feel after their loved ones or friends pass away. ALFs provide a ready-made peer group, in-house activities and trips to various community events. Some ALFs also provide transportation for shopping and doctor appointments. Many even have an on-site pet!

Two recent trends in Assisted Living:

1) Offering "Independent Living" - People move into an Assisted Living Facility before needing any assistance. They enjoy a beautiful apartment, recreation opportunities, good meals and are around their age group. They can "age in place" – stay in the same unit when they begin to need help with the ADLs.

Assisted Living regularly monitors their residents' ability to do the ADLs, even residents in independent living situations, and can communicate that status with family.

2) Residents are able to stay in the Assisted Living Facility until the end of their lives. More Assisted Living Facilities are providing a higher level of medical care and many are licensed to provide hospice care. Years ago, people needing help with more than a few of the ADLs or those with a chronic medical issue would be transferred to a Nursing Home.

A special note should be made that Assisted Living Facilities can also offer special housing sections for those suffering from severe cognitive impairment. There are also facilities that specialize in dementia care.

Home Care and Care in the Community

80% of us get long term care at home or in the community.

Care at home comes in two flavors: home care and home health care. Even though the two differ by just one word it is a huge difference. Home care is not trying to cure us or make us better. Home care is just providing basic assistance with ADLs, just the basic care to keep us alive. It is similar to the care we give kids when they are very young. Examples are helping someone wash his or her hair, get dressed or get in or out of a bed or chair. Not exciting or glamorous work.

There are two types of home care: formal and informal. Formal home care typically is provided by someone from a company. Informal home care is given by someone not from a company (examples: spouse, siblings, kids, neighbor etc.). Informal home care providers can receive pay for their service. Of note, most home care given in the U.S. is informal home care.

Home health care is care that is trying to cure us. A RN, LVN, occupational therapist or physical therapist works with the patient during a short visit. A home health care visit does not involve help with doing laundry, cooking, cleaning or shopping.

Most health insurance policies (and Medicare) provide very limited coverage for home health care and do not cover home care at all.

If home care is your plan you have to decide between hiring a Home Care agency to provide a caregiver or hiring someone yourself. There are key advantages to using an agency:

1) They screen their employees, who are often bonded, in turn giving assurance to clients they

do not have a questionable background.

2) The agency handles all taxes.

3) The agency trains the caregivers and makes sure they are able to provide the needed care (for example, they are strong enough to pick up a client if needed).

4) If you do not like the caregiver, you call the agency and have a new caregiver sent over. Compare this to how unpleasant it might be to fire a friend or relative that you have hired as a caregiver.

5) Most people would not want a relative or friend to see them naked or help them with going to the bathroom.

Adult Day Care

Care in the community refers to Adult Day Care. These centers provide an opportunity for care outside home during normal workday hours and are usually open Monday through Friday. Almost 80% are non-profit and almost 70% are part of a larger organization.

There are two "models" or types of Adult Day Care – social model and medical model. Both provide meals, and help with Activities of Daily Living, transportation to and from the facility and social activities. Medical model centers also provide medical care like short-term therapy for someone recently discharged from the hospital or care for chronic conditions.

Complete information on Adult Daycare Center can be found at the website of the National Adult Day Services Association at *www.nasda.org*.

Respite Care

Respite Care is when a regular caregiver gets a short-term break. It can mean either a Home Care agency takes over at home or the person getting care goes to an Assisted Living Facility, Nursing Home or Adult Daycare Center.

Respite Care can be one-time or recurring and last from a few days up to a few months. Here are creative examples of using Respite Care:

1) A few weeks each year when the family goes camping.

2) When the family home is being remodeled and the construction in the house make it hard for the care recipient.

3) To allow a family to "test" the idea of using an Adult Day care or an Assisted Living Facility or care in their home from a non-family member.

Hospice

The end of a loved one's life affects not only the caregiver but also the entire family of the patient.

The first thing to learn about Hospice is that it is a type of care that can be received at home, hospital, nursing home, assisted living facility or a standalone Hospice facility. It is typically for people who are expected to have less than 6 months to live. Hospice care does not try to keep the person alive but focuses on relieving the chronic pain that terminally ill people often experience.

Health insurance and Medicare cover hospice care. The family doctor remains involved with the patient and their family while the patient is receiving Hospice.

It is important to understand that hospice care is typically skilled care and does not help in one's home with Activities of Daily Living. Of course, hospice care in a facility provides help with the Activities of Daily Living.

For more information, visit *www.hospicefoundation.org/whatishospice.*

CHAPTER FOUR:
Who Pays For Long Term Care?

Key to understanding who pays for Long Term Care is realizing the difference between Skilled Care and Unskilled Care (also called custodial care).

Skilled Care is trying to cure and thus make us better; it is the care we get from someone with a medical license (doctor, nurse, x-ray tech, respiratory and occupational therapists etc.)

Unskilled Care is not trying to cure us but rather just helps us live each day. It is basically providing help with the Activities of Daily Living, something that we cannot live without.

Health Insurance

Health insurance does not cover long term care.

Health insurance pays to cure us (skilled care) with care provided by someone with a license: physicians, nurses, physical therapists, respiratory therapists, x-ray technicians and pharmacists.

Since most long term care is unskilled care or custodial care, health insurance does not cover it. The "exclusions" section in your health insurance policy contains the actual wording showing the policy does not cover long term care. Here are examples of actual wording from health insurance policies excluding long term care:

- "Exclusions: Custodial care"
- "Medical care not covered: Custodial Care or Rest Cures."
- "Exclusions: Custodial care, except for covered hospice care."

Example 1: Susan, a 45-year-old law firm administrator, goes skiing and hits a tree breaking both legs and her right arm. Her health insurance pays for:

- Ambulance from ski resort to hospital
- MRI
- Hospital bed for four days
- Surgeon and Anesthesiologist
- Titanium plates and screws that are inserted into broken limbs
- Body cast
- Ambulance from hospital to Susan's home

So far, so good! Her health insurance covers $320,000 worth of bills.

She is sent home from the hospital in body cast. An hour after getting home, she has to use the bathroom - a real problem when you are in a body cast and are alone at home. Using her one good arm, she calls her health insurance carrier and asks them to send someone into her home and help her. She learns that help at home with the Activities of Daily Living is not covered by health insurance because it is unskilled care or custodial care. Susan ends up paying out of her own pocket for someone to come to her house each day and help her for the six months she is in the body cast.

Medicare

Medicare is health insurance from the federal government for Americans aged 65 and older. Since Medicare is health insurance, it does not cover long term care. Medicare is very confusing and the rules seem to change all the time.

Medicare has four "parts":

- Part A is often called "hospital insurance" and covers part of the costs for care in a hospital and rehab facility.

- Part B is called "medical insurance" and helps cover doctor bills and outpatient care.
- Part C is commonly referred to as "Medicare Advantage" and consists of Part A and Part B coverage from a Medicare approved private sector provider.
- Part D provides some coverage for Prescription Drugs. You pay for Part D unless you are in a Part C/Medicare Advantage plan that covers prescription drugs.

We already know that the vast majority of long term care is unskilled care or custodial care – so it is NOT covered by Medicare. In fact, the Medicare website states:

"Medicare doesn't cover custodial care if it is the only kind of care you need."

To make things confusing, Medicare can cover part of the cost for a limited stay in a nursing home. Medicare can cover up to 100 days in a year in a Nursing Home if

1) The patient first spends at least three days in a hospital and

2) The patient improves every consecutive day in the Nursing Home for the next 100 days.

The first day the patient does not improve Medicare ends the claim for the year. This is because the first day the patient does not improve they turn into a "custodial" or "unskilled" patient and Medicare does not cover that. Typically, Medicare only pays for about 21 days a year for Nursing Home care. On day 22 the patient is still in need of care but Medicare has ended the claim because the patient did not improve on day 21.

Please note that it is very likely that someone will still need lots of help once Medicare stops paying for Nursing Home care.

How much can Medicare pay for covered nursing home care?

Medicare pays 100% of the cost for the first 20 days of a covered nursing home stay. The patient then pays a co-pay for the remaining days until they reach 100 days in the facility which is the maximum possible benefit for care; then Medicare ends the claim and the patient either pays the entire daily bill for the care themselves or they go home.

Complete information on Medicare can be found at www.medicare.gov.

Long Term Care Insurance

Everyone should try to get a long term care insurance policy. Everyone. It can make the difference in how your later years turn out. In 2010, long term care insurance companies paid an estimated $6 billion dollars in claims.

The Federal government, most Fortune 500 firms, state governments and major cities offer group long term care insurance plans to their employees. (Happily, I helped implement many of those plans by doing the employee education component.)

There are two types of traditional long term care insurance policies:

1)   Plans that only cover care in a facility (Assisted Living or Nursing Home) that are called Facility Only policies. Please note these plans do not cover care at home.

2)   Comprehensive Policies cover care in a facility or care in the insured's own home or community and these are the most popular type of policy. (The client always chooses the setting for care when they go on claim).

Today, almost all long term care insurance policies include the services of a "care advocate" who is a nurse or social worker who helps the client make decisions about their care.

The two key long term care insurance concepts are:

1) "Pool of money" or "lifetime maximum benefit" and

2) "Daily benefit amount".

The "pool of money" or "lifetime maximum benefit" is the maximum amount of care your policy will pay for over the life of the contract. This total amount of benefit is even available if you need to make a claim the first day your policy is effective.

The daily benefit amount is the maximum that your policy will pay for care each day.

Almost every adult already has one or more "pools of money" from an insurance company. Examples include the face value of life insurance and the policy limits on car and homeowners insurance.

A long term care insurance policy pays for care until you use up the entire amount of the "pool of money" or lifetime maximum benefit you bought with the plan. If you spend less than the maximum daily benefit amount, then your plan will pay longer for your care.

There is much confusion about what a

long term care insurance policy costs and what constitutes the "perfect policy" for someone. The cost for a long term care insurance policy is very simple – you buy a policy that fits your monthly budget. If you want a policy and you can afford $120 per month then you should get a $120 policy. Of course, the more you spend for your policy the more benefit you get.

The "perfect policy" for someone is easy to figure out. The "perfect policy" is the policy someone already has in place when something happens to him or her.

Example: a 45-year-old woman is paralyzed in a car accident. She has a long term care insurance policy with a "pool of money" or lifetime maximum benefit of $185,000. This policy is the perfect policy for her because she had the policy in effect when she was injured.

Think of it this way: a person with three small kids dies unexpectedly with only $100,000 in life insurance. Would the surviving spouse refuse the check for $100,000 saying, "This amount is not enough?" No, the surviving spouse would be very grateful for the $100,000. Of course, more life insurance benefit would be better for their kids, but no one would refuse what help already exists.

If you were drowning in a flood, would you

turn down the help of rescuers in a rowboat because you prefer to be rescued by a huge Coast Guard vessel? No, you would be very happy the rowboat was there to save you.

Are these examples absurd? No, because this is the same thinking people display when they do not get any long term care insurance policy because they cannot afford a huge and expensive policy.

Remember, most women ultimately need long term care. Without long term care insurance they risk using up all their own money and going broke.

In past years, some respected financial and consumer resources have given the insane advice that people should wait to apply for long term care insurance until they get a serious condition or turn 65. This is equivalent to suggesting that people wait until their home catches fire before they try to get homeowner insurance or suggesting people wait until they get terminally ill before trying to get life insurance. One couple I met relied upon flawed advice and put off getting long term care insurance until they turned 65. Unfortunately, the husband had a stroke before turning 65 and his application was denied.

There are exciting new products coming out from insurance companies that provide additional ways to address long term care costs. New life insurance polices are available that include a long term care benefit. You can definitely get your money's worth with one of these new "hybrid" policies.

Disability Insurance

Short-Term Disability Insurance and Long-Term Disability Insurance do not pay for long term care.

Disability Insurance is "paycheck insurance." It replaces part of your paycheck (50% to 66%) if you are unable to work. Disability insurance does not typically pay to have someone take care of you.

Example: Jane is a 27-year-old airline pilot in San Jose, CA. On weekends she rides her bike to the ocean.

One weekend Jane falls off her bike and ruptures three disks in her spine. After surgery, Jane contracts a serious post-operative infection and misses eight months of work.

Her disability insurance replaces 66% of her pay each month. While recovering at home she needs help with the Activities of Daily Living. She has to pay out of her own pocket for someone to come to her apartment each day and care for her.

Medicaid

Medicaid is a government program that does pay for long term care and actually pays for about half of all long term care in the U.S. It is a joint federal and state program providing health insurance for low income individuals and families.

There are three problems with relying on Medicaid to pay for our long term care. The first problem with relying on Medicaid to pay for our long term care is that Medicaid is health insurance. We already know health insurance is not designed to cover long term care.

Medicaid typically only pays for long term care in a nursing home. Home Care and Assisted Living are typically NOT covered. Since it is a joint federal and state program, there are variations in what Medicaid covers in each state.

The second problem is that Medicaid is intended for low income people. We typically have to be broke or pretty close to it to qualify for Medicaid long term care benefits. Medicaid will not pay for nursing home care if we have more than $2,000 in assets. Your primary residence is usually not counted if you intend to return home after recovery and your home equity does not exceed $500,000. States can raise the equity limit to $750,000.

There is also a monthly income limit to be eligible for Medicaid to pay for our Nursing Home care. Currently it is $60 a month for personal needs. Therefore, someone getting a monthly check from Social Security would have to turn his or her entire check over to the nursing home except for the $60.

Married couples do not have to use up all their resources to qualify for Medicaid. There is "protection" for the healthy spouse so they do not have to become impoverished. The healthy spouse can keep 50% of the couple's assets, up to a limit of $109,000.

The third problem with relying on Medicaid to pay for your long term care costs is Asset Recovery. Federal law requires state Medicaid programs to try to get paid back, or recover, for the benefits that Medicaid pays out for long term care costs. Medicaid will try to "recover" the benefit dollars from the estate, or property, or the person who received the Medicaid benefits. The state puts a "lien" or financial claim on assets, including real estate, owned by the Medicaid benefit recipient. The state will need to get repaid for the Medicaid benefits paid out before anyone else can receive any assets that belong to the Medicaid recipient.

Example: Betty is an 80 year old widow who lives on a 1200 acre ranch just north of Spearfish, South Dakota. She lives on her Social Security benefits and rent from her land. She eventually needs care in a Nursing Home and uses up all her savings. Her monthly Social Security benefits and rent do not cover the monthly cost for the Nursing Home. Betty is able to apply for Medicaid to cover her Nursing Home bills even though she still owns her home on the 1200 acres (because she intends to return to her home if she ever recovers). However, once Betty is approved for Medicaid benefits to pay for her Nursing Home the state Medicaid office places a lien on her property. If that property is sold while Betty is alive the state must be repaid for any Medicaid benefits Betty has received.

After Betty passes away, the state will have to be repaid for the dollars Medicaid has spent for her care before any of her assets can be distributed to her beneficiaries.

You cannot give away assets to qualify for Medicaid. Federal law requires each state Medicaid office to ensure no assets were transferred or given away in the five years before someone applies for Medicaid. This is called the "look back period" and Medicaid agencies are very good at discovering evidence of asset transfer. The penalty for transferring assets is being ineligible for Medicaid benefits for a period of time corresponding to the amount of assets that you transferred.

More details on Medicaid can be obtained from your state's Department of Social Services.

Chapter Five:
Geriatric Care Manager

The challenges:
- You live in one state and the person who needs care or help with their affairs is in another state.
- You want an impartial expert to occasionally check on your loved one and assess their health or living conditions.
- You are already overwhelmed with your work and family responsibilities and want someone else to take over your care giving or decision making responsibilities.
- You and your siblings are constantly at odds concerning care for your loved one. You desperately need an impartial expert to step in and offer expert advice.

The solution is a Geriatric Care Manager (GCM). They are possibly the best resource available for people giving or getting care and come from a variety of backgrounds including nursing, social work, physical, speech, and occupational therapy, and mental health.
Geriatric Care Managers are experts in

assessing or evaluating the need for care and determining where that care is best provided and who might pay for the services.

Example: Your mom breaks her hip and is hospitalized. The Geriatric Care Manager comes to your mom's hospital room and you have him or her:

- Monitor your mom's care in the hospital.
- Assist you in selecting the nursing home your mom will go to after her hospital stay.
- Be at the nursing home when your mom is admitted and then serve as liaison with the nursing home staff.
- Help you and your mom plan for her return home and determine if your mom needs home care and equipment like a hospital bed.
- Arrange any required home care and perform a home safety check.
- Monitor your mom's home care and health.

Example: Carol, a 75-year-old woman, lives with her 82-year-old husband Bob. Carol falls, breaks her hip and will be out of their home for weeks.

Carol's daughter is a dentist in private practice, living 900 miles away. The daughter arranges for a Geriatric Care Manager who:

- Evaluates the family and home situation in place before Carol breaks her hip. The Geriatric Care Manager asks, "Was Carol helping anyone?" It turns out that Carol was managing medications for her husband and someone will need to do that while Carol is hospitalized.
- Checks in on both Carol and Bob. She arranges for a home care provider to come in daily to cook meals for Bob and make sure he is taking his medication.

The ideal situation is for us to talk to a Geriatric Care Manager well before any crisis hits. It may feel awkward suggesting to your parents that they meet with a Geriatric Care Manager to discuss how to prepare for things that might happen in the future. However, it might turn out to be a huge relief for all involved to have a discussion with an expert guide.

Geriatric Care Managers perform evaluations (also called assessments) of individuals who may be in need of care. It can be as basic assessment or a full assessment. A basic assessment usually includes:

1) Physical ability – Can the person perform the ADLs and how is their overall mobility?
2) Cognition – Does the person appear to have some sort of cognitive impairment?
3) Location – Is the home hazard free, clean and in good condition? What support currently exists?

If key warning signs appear during a basic assessment a full assessment is performed. With a full assessment, the Geriatric Care Manager visits more than once and at different times of day and includes conversations with other family members, caregivers and medical providers. This helps the Geriatric Care Manager in obtaining a complete picture of the situation. Multiple visits at a variety of times are also important because:

1) They offer a better chance to see the real condition of the person (it is difficult for people to hide cognitive conditions over a long period of time). It is not uncommon to discover someone who appears fine during the first visit, however, has not changed their clothes by the second visit. Multiple visits also give the chance to check if the patient has refilled prescriptions or is contradicting earlier statements.
2) People can function differently at various times of day. Some people may be able to do all

the ADLs in the morning but not later in the day when a physical condition like arthritis may slow them down. Also, many types of severe cognitive impairments get worse starting in the late afternoon and going into the evening, something called "sun downing".

You can find out more about Geriatric Care Managers, and get a list of licensed professionals, at their national association: *http://www.caremanager.org.*

Chapter Six:
Legal Considerations

Everyone should spend an hour talking to an Elder Law or Probate attorney. This first meeting, called an initial consultation, could potentially spare your family thousands of dollars in unnecessary expenses and much heartache.

An Elder Law or Probate attorney can help us plan for two separate and critical phases of our lives. The first phase is a potential period in our life when we are unable to care for ourselves or are unable to make decisions about our medical care or finances. The second phase is the "probate phase" or the time after we have passed away.

Example: A 65-year-old woman falls on her icy driveway and is in a coma. Her family rushes to the hospital and is met by a series of questions from the medical staff about what kinds of treatments the injured women would want administered.

Without advance legal planning, family members may be asked to answer detailed questions about the direction of medical treatments that they cannot answer. Even if family members know the desires of the injured person, they may not have the legal authority to make decisions for the injured person.

The following information is not intended to be legal advice and it must be noted that the laws vary in each state.

There are two situations in which we can obtain the legal authority to make decisions for a loved one:

1) Power of Attorney - The ideal situation is before something happens when the person is still of sound mind and they willingly give us the power to make decisions for them. This situation is called a Power of Attorney

2) Conservatorship or Guardianship - The less desirable situation is after something happens and the person we want to help is not able to make a competent decision.

An "immediate" Power of Attorney means that once the forms are signed, the person who was granted the Power of Attorney can begin making decisions. This would be appropriate for someone scheduled for major brain surgery - in case the surgery goes bad and decisions have to be made about life-sustaining actions.

The other type of Power of Attorney takes effect only after a specific triggering event takes place. The triggering event is described in detail in the application for Power of Attorney. For example, a person with a diagnosis of Alzheimer's might complete paperwork for Power of Attorney that will allow their daughter to make decisions for them once two physicians determine they are no longer capable to make their own decisions.

There are typically two separate areas covered by a Power of Attorney: Power of Attorney for the Person and a Power of Attorney for the Estate. Either individual can have the responsibility for both areas or two different persons can handle them.

The Power of Attorney for the Person allows decisions to be made regarding issues like health care and living arrangements. The Power of Attorney for the Estate allows financial decisions. This Power of Attorney allows someone to become a signer on the patient's checking account and liquidate assets to pay for their health care bills and other expenses.

A person who holds any Power of Attorney is held by the court granting the Power of Attorney to a standard of conduct of acting in the best interest of the person who gave the Power of Attorney (this is commonly referred to as a "fiduciary duty"). This duty is what is supposed to stop an adult child from spending all their parents' money.

Conservatorship is the other, far less desirable, method for obtaining the legal authority to make decisions for someone. This is the required route when no advanced planning has taken place and someone is no longer mentally capable of making their own decisions. Arranging a Conservatorship can take months and can be very expensive and someone will have to pay the attorney and court costs up front.

In Conservatorship, the first step is for a petition to be filed with the Probate Court. The petition names the person who needs help, called the Conservatee, and the person who wants the power to make decisions and the legal reasons for needing Conservatorship. The person asking for the Conservatorship will usually need to include medical statements from attending physicians attesting to the Conservatee's medical condition and how those conditions prevent the Conservatee from being able to handle their own affairs.

Once the petition is filed, the Court then sends out an investigator to visit the person who supposedly cannot care for themselves along with their medical providers. The investigator reports the results of their investigation to the Court.

Example: Someone has a major stroke and is in a permanent vegetative state and one of their adult kids files a petition for Conservatorship. The investigator from the Court would go to the person's hospital bed to make sure the person is, indeed, laying there in a vegetative state as described in the petition. At the end of the investigative process, the judge holds a hearing and issues a ruling whether or not to grant the Conservatorship.

One way Conservatorship is different from Power of Attorney in that a Conservator has to make periodic reports to the court about his or her activities. Conservators are usually family members but someone else can fill that role also. A family might want a professional like a CPA or Geriatric Care Manger to be the Conservator. This could be appropriate when no family member lives nearby or no family member wants the responsibility.

Conservatorship has two types: Conservatorship of the Person and Conservatorship of the Estate and one person can fill both positions.

We can try to avoid being kept alive for months or years at the end of our lives hooked up machines in two ways. The first is to set up at Power of Attorney and make sure the person you name in the Power of Attorney knows what your specific desires are (like your desire to have a feeding tube, surgeries or narcotics for pain relief etc.).

The second way typically involves your health care providers. You can tell your personal physician your wishes in writing. If you are hospitalized, you can fill out an "advance medical directive" that will instruct the hospital and staff about your wishes regarding surgical complications and issuance of a "Do Not Resuscitate" (DNR) order. Since there is an ever increasing variety of "life sustaining measures," many hospitals have begun using a new form called a "POLST" which stands for Physician Orders for Life Sustaining Treatments. It goes into detail on specific treatments one does or does not want.

Here are places to look for an attorney:

- The National Academy of Elder Law Attorneys
- The American Association of Estate Planning Attorneys
- Your local county Bar Association

Chapter Seven:
Conclusion And Review

What is long term care?

We now know that there are two separate causes or "triggers" for a long term care situation.

One cause is physical limitations that will prevent us from being able to fully care for ourselves, the other is severe cognitive impairment that will make us a threat to ourselves and others. Physical limitation and cognitive impairment both have to be expected to last at least 90 days.

Where do we get long term care?

Long term care is received in three different places or "settings". The settings are in our own home or the community (Adult Day Care), in an Assisted Living Facility or a Nursing Home. We are most likely to receive long term care in our own home or in our community (80% of the time).

Who pays for long term care?

The key concept is understanding the distinction between Skilled Care and Unskilled Care (custodial care). Health insurance plans pay for Skilled Care that is trying to cure us and is provided by licensed medical personnel such as a doctor, nurse, or physical therapist. Unskilled Care or custodial care is not covered by health insurance plans and is care that does not try to cure us but helps us stay alive and includes help with Activities of Daily Living.

Health insurance plans, Medicare and Disability insurance do not pay for long term care. Medicaid can pay for care in a nursing home if we are impoverished.

Long term care insurance is the only thing that is designed to cover long term care costs. It is highly recommended to get a long term care policy before we actually need it. The "perfect plan" is the plan that we have in place when we need care.

We should all have a consultation, as soon as possible, with a Geriatric Care Manager, an insurance agent and an Elder Law or Probate attorney. These professionals can help us make plans and arrangements today that can save us and our families much money and turmoil later.

Remember, things rarely get easier if we put them off!

The Essential Long Term Care & Elder Care Handbook:

By Don Grimes
© 2011 Don Grimes

www.ingramcontent.com/pod-product-compliance
Lightning Source LLC
Chambersburg PA
CBHW070519090426
42735CB00012B/2843